PASSWORD
LOGBOOK

NAME:

PHONE:

ADRESS:

CHOOSING A GOOD PASSWORD.

THE LONGER, THE BETTER! MAKE YOUR PASSWORDS

AT LEAST 12 CHARACTERS IN LENGTH.

MAKE THEM UNIQUE! MAKE EACH PASSWORD

YOU CREATE DIFFERENTLY.

MIX IT UP! USE A MIXTURE OF CAPITALS, DIGITS & SYMBOLS.

A TOP TIP IS TO USE SEVERAL RANDOM WORDS

TOGETHER TO CREATE AN AMUSING, MEMORABLE

IMAGE. IT IS A GOOD IDEA TO AVOID OBVIOUSLY

REFERENCES, SUCH AS BIRTHDAYS & ANNIVERSARIES OR

SOMETHING THAT IS OBVIOUS TO THE WEBSITE ITSELF.

THE BEST PASSWORDS ARE COMPLETELY RANDOM, THIS

TYPE OF PASSWORD, HOWEVER, IS HARD TO

REMEMBER, SO STORE THEM IN THIS HANDY BOOK &

YOU WILL HAVE THEM TO HAND WHEN YOU NEED THEM.

HOME NETWORK SETTINGS

BROADBAND MODEM:
MODEL:
SERIAL NUMBER:
MAC ADDRESS:
ADMINISTRATION URL/IP ADDRESS:
WAN IP ADDRESS:
USERNAME:
PASSWORD:
ROUTER/WIRELESS ACCESS POINT:
MODEL:
SERIAL NUMBER:
DEFAULT IP ADDRESS:
DEFAULT USERNAME:
DEFAULT PASSWORD:
USER DEFINED IP ADDRESS:
USER DEFINED USERNAME:
USER DEFINED PASSWORD:
WAN SETTINGS:
MAC ADDRESS:
PASSWORD:
PASSWORD:

| IP ADDRESS: |
| HOST NAME: |
| DOMAIN NAME: |
| SUBNET MASK: |
| DEFAULT GATEWAY: |
| DNS --PRIMARY: |
| DNS -- SECONDARY |
| LAN SETTINGS |
| IP ADDRESS: |
| SUBNET MASK: |
| DHCP RANGE: |
| WIRELESS SETTINGS: |
| SSID (NETWORK NAME): |
| CHANNEL: |
| SECURITY MODE: |
| SHARED KEY (WPA): |
| PASSPHRASE (WEP): |

INTERNET & COMPUTER INFORMATION

ISP NAME:	
ACCOUNT NUMBER:	
TECH SUPPORT:	
CUSTOMER SERVICE:	
EMAIL (PERSONAL):	
MAIL SERVER TYPE:	
INCOMING SERVER:	
OUTGOING SERVER:	
USERNAME:	
PASSWORD:	
EMAIL (WORK):	
MAIL SERVER TYPE:	
INCOMING SERVER:	
OUTGOING SERVER:	

A

B

C

D

E

F

G

H

I

J

K

L

M

N

O

P

Q

R

S

T

U

V

W

X

Y

Z

WEBSITE:

USERNAME:

PASSWORD:

PASSWORD:

EMAIL:

NOTES:

WEBSITE:

USERNAME:

PASSWORD:

PASSWORD:

EMAIL:

NOTES:

WEBSITE:

USERNAME:

PASSWORD:

PASSWORD:

EMAIL:

NOTES:

WEBSITE:

USERNAME:

PASSWORD:

PASSWORD:

EMAIL:

NOTES:

WEBSITE:

USERNAME:

PASSWORD:

PASSWORD:

EMAIL:

NOTES:

WEBSITE:

USERNAME:

PASSWORD:

PASSWORD:

EMAIL:

NOTES:

WEBSITE:

USERNAME:

PASSWORD:

PASSWORD:

EMAIL:

NOTES:

WEBSITE:

USERNAME:

PASSWORD:

PASSWORD:

EMAIL:

NOTES:

WEBSITE:

USERNAME:

PASSWORD:

PASSWORD:

EMAIL:

NOTES:

WEBSITE:

USERNAME:

PASSWORD:

PASSWORD:

EMAIL:

NOTES:

WEBSITE:

USERNAME:

PASSWORD:

PASSWORD:

EMAIL:

NOTES:

WEBSITE:

USERNAME:

PASSWORD:

PASSWORD:

EMAIL:

NOTES:

A
B
C
D
E
F
G
H
I
J
K
L
M
N
O
P
Q
R
S
T
U
V
W
X
Y
Z

WEBSITE:

USERNAME:

PASSWORD:

PASSWORD:

EMAIL:

NOTES:

WEBSITE:

USERNAME:

PASSWORD:

PASSWORD:

EMAIL:

NOTES:

WEBSITE:

USERNAME:

PASSWORD:

PASSWORD:

EMAIL:

NOTES:

WEBSITE:

USERNAME:

PASSWORD:

PASSWORD:

EMAIL:

NOTES:

WEBSITE:

USERNAME:

PASSWORD:

PASSWORD:

EMAIL:

NOTES:

WEBSITE:

USERNAME:

PASSWORD:

PASSWORD:

EMAIL:

NOTES:

A B C D E F G H I J K L M N O P Q R S T U V W X Y Z

A
B
C
D
E
F
G
H
I
J
K
L
M
N
O
P
Q
R
S
T
U
V
W
X
Y
Z

WEBSITE:

USERNAME:

PASSWORD:

PASSWORD:

EMAIL:

NOTES:

WEBSITE:

USERNAME:

PASSWORD:

PASSWORD:

EMAIL:

NOTES:

WEBSITE:

USERNAME:

PASSWORD:

PASSWORD:

EMAIL:

NOTES:

WEBSITE:

USERNAME:

PASSWORD:

PASSWORD:

EMAIL:

NOTES:

WEBSITE:

USERNAME:

PASSWORD:

PASSWORD:

EMAIL:

NOTES:

WEBSITE:

USERNAME:

PASSWORD:

PASSWORD:

EMAIL:

NOTES:

A B C D E F G H I J K L M N O P Q R S T U V W X Y Z

<table>
<tr><td rowspan="26" style="vertical-align:top">A
B
C
D
E
F
G
H
I
J
K
L
M
N
O
P
Q
R
S
T
U
V
W
X
Y
Z</td></tr>
</table>

WEBSITE:

USERNAME:

PASSWORD:

PASSWORD:

EMAIL:

NOTES:

WEBSITE:

USERNAME:

PASSWORD:

PASSWORD:

EMAIL:

NOTES:

WEBSITE:

USERNAME:

PASSWORD:

PASSWORD:

EMAIL:

NOTES:

WEBSITE:

USERNAME:

PASSWORD:

PASSWORD:

EMAIL:

NOTES:

WEBSITE:

USERNAME:

PASSWORD:

PASSWORD:

EMAIL:

NOTES:

WEBSITE:

USERNAME:

PASSWORD:

PASSWORD:

EMAIL:

NOTES:

A
B
C
D
E
F
G
H
I
J
K
L
M
N
O
P
Q
R
S
T
U
V
W
X
Y
Z

WEBSITE:

USERNAME:

PASSWORD:

PASSWORD:

EMAIL:

NOTES:

WEBSITE:

USERNAME:

PASSWORD:

PASSWORD:

EMAIL:

NOTES:

WEBSITE:

USERNAME:

PASSWORD:

PASSWORD:

EMAIL:

NOTES:

WEBSITE:

USERNAME:

PASSWORD:

PASSWORD:

EMAIL:

NOTES:

WEBSITE:

USERNAME:

PASSWORD:

PASSWORD:

EMAIL:

NOTES:

WEBSITE:

USERNAME:

PASSWORD:

PASSWORD:

EMAIL:

NOTES:

A
B
C
D
E
F
G
H
I
J
K
L
M
N
O
P
Q
R
S
T
U
V
W
X
Y
Z

A
B
C
D
E
F
G
H
I
J
K
L
M
N
O
P
Q
R
S
T
U
V
W
X
Y
Z

WEBSITE:

USERNAME:

PASSWORD:

PASSWORD:

EMAIL:

NOTES:

WEBSITE:

USERNAME:

PASSWORD:

PASSWORD:

EMAIL:

NOTES:

WEBSITE:

USERNAME:

PASSWORD:

PASSWORD:

EMAIL:

NOTES:

WEBSITE:

USERNAME:

PASSWORD:

PASSWORD:

EMAIL:

NOTES:

WEBSITE:

USERNAME:

PASSWORD:

PASSWORD:

EMAIL:

NOTES:

WEBSITE:

USERNAME:

PASSWORD:

PASSWORD:

EMAIL:

NOTES:

A
B
C
D
E
F
G
H
I
J
K
L
M
N
O
P
Q
R
S
T
U
V
W
X
Y
Z

A
B
C
D
E
F
G
H
I
J
K
L
M
N
O
P
Q
R
S
T
U
V
W
X
Y
Z

WEBSITE:

USERNAME:

PASSWORD:

PASSWORD:

EMAIL:

NOTES:

WEBSITE:

USERNAME:

PASSWORD:

PASSWORD:

EMAIL:

NOTES:

WEBSITE:

USERNAME:

PASSWORD:

PASSWORD:

EMAIL:

NOTES:

WEBSITE:

USERNAME:

PASSWORD:

PASSWORD:

EMAIL:

NOTES:

WEBSITE:

USERNAME:

PASSWORD:

PASSWORD:

EMAIL:

NOTES:

WEBSITE:

USERNAME:

PASSWORD:

PASSWORD:

EMAIL:

NOTES:

A
B
C
D
E
F
G
H
I
J
K
L
M
N
O
P
Q
R
S
T
U
V
W
X
Y
Z

A
B
C
D
E
F
G
H
I
J
K
L
M
N
O
P
Q
R
S
T
U
V
W
X
Y
Z

WEBSITE:

USERNAME:

PASSWORD:

PASSWORD:

EMAIL:

NOTES:

WEBSITE:

USERNAME:

PASSWORD:

PASSWORD:

EMAIL:

NOTES:

WEBSITE:

USERNAME:

PASSWORD:

PASSWORD:

EMAIL:

NOTES:

WEBSITE:

USERNAME:

PASSWORD:

PASSWORD:

EMAIL:

NOTES:

WEBSITE:

USERNAME:

PASSWORD:

PASSWORD:

EMAIL:

NOTES:

WEBSITE:

USERNAME:

PASSWORD:

PASSWORD:

EMAIL:

NOTES:

<table>
<tr><td rowspan="26">A
B
C
D
E
F
G
H
I
J
K
L
M
N
O
P
Q
R
S
T
U
V
W
X
Y
Z</td></tr>
</table>

WEBSITE:

USERNAME:

PASSWORD:

PASSWORD:

EMAIL:

NOTES:

WEBSITE:

USERNAME:

PASSWORD:

PASSWORD:

EMAIL:

NOTES:

WEBSITE:

USERNAME:

PASSWORD:

PASSWORD:

EMAIL:

NOTES:

WEBSITE:	
USERNAME:	
PASSWORD:	
PASSWORD:	
EMAIL:	
NOTES:	

WEBSITE:	
USERNAME:	
PASSWORD:	
PASSWORD:	
EMAIL:	
NOTES:	

WEBSITE:	
USERNAME:	
PASSWORD:	
PASSWORD:	
EMAIL:	
NOTES:	

<table>
<tr><td>A
B
C
D
E
F
G
H
I
J
K
L
M
N
O
P
Q
R
S
T
U
V
W
X
Y
Z</td><td>

WEBSITE:

USERNAME:

PASSWORD:

PASSWORD:

EMAIL:

NOTES:

WEBSITE:

USERNAME:

PASSWORD:

PASSWORD:

EMAIL:

NOTES:

WEBSITE:

USERNAME:

PASSWORD:

PASSWORD:

EMAIL:

NOTES:

</td></tr>
</table>

WEBSITE:

USERNAME:

PASSWORD:

PASSWORD:

EMAIL:

NOTES:

WEBSITE:

USERNAME:

PASSWORD:

PASSWORD:

EMAIL:

NOTES:

WEBSITE:

USERNAME:

PASSWORD:

PASSWORD:

EMAIL:

NOTES:

A B C D E F G H I J K L M N O P Q R S T U V W X Y Z

A
B
C
D
E
F
G
H
I
J
K
L
M
N
O
P
Q
R
S
T
U
V
W
X
Y
Z

WEBSITE:

USERNAME:

PASSWORD:

PASSWORD:

EMAIL:

NOTES:

WEBSITE:

USERNAME:

PASSWORD:

PASSWORD:

EMAIL:

NOTES:

WEBSITE:

USERNAME:

PASSWORD:

PASSWORD:

EMAIL:

NOTES:

WEBSITE:	
USERNAME:	
PASSWORD:	
PASSWORD:	
EMAIL:	
NOTES:	

WEBSITE:	
USERNAME:	
PASSWORD:	
PASSWORD:	
EMAIL:	
NOTES:	

WEBSITE:	
USERNAME:	
PASSWORD:	
PASSWORD:	
EMAIL:	
NOTES:	

A B C D E **F** G H I J K L M N O P Q R S T U V W X Y Z

A
B
C
D
E
F
G
H
I
J
K
L
M
N
O
P
Q
R
S
T
U
V
W
X
Y
Z

WEBSITE:

USERNAME:

PASSWORD:

PASSWORD:

EMAIL:

NOTES:

WEBSITE:

USERNAME:

PASSWORD:

PASSWORD:

EMAIL:

NOTES:

WEBSITE:

USERNAME:

PASSWORD:

PASSWORD:

EMAIL:

NOTES:

WEBSITE:

USERNAME:

PASSWORD:

PASSWORD:

EMAIL:

NOTES:

WEBSITE:

USERNAME:

PASSWORD:

PASSWORD:

EMAIL:

NOTES:

WEBSITE:

USERNAME:

PASSWORD:

PASSWORD:

EMAIL:

NOTES:

A
B
C
D
E
F
G
H
I
J
K
L
M
N
O
P
Q
R
S
T
U
V
W
X
Y
Z

WEBSITE:

USERNAME:

PASSWORD:

PASSWORD:

EMAIL:

NOTES:

WEBSITE:

USERNAME:

PASSWORD:

PASSWORD:

EMAIL:

NOTES:

WEBSITE:

USERNAME:

PASSWORD:

PASSWORD:

EMAIL:

NOTES:

| WEBSITE: |
| USERNAME: |
| PASSWORD: |
| PASSWORD: |
| EMAIL: |
| NOTES: |

| WEBSITE: |
| USERNAME: |
| PASSWORD: |
| PASSWORD: |
| EMAIL: |
| NOTES: |

| WEBSITE: |
| USERNAME: |
| PASSWORD: |
| PASSWORD: |
| EMAIL: |
| NOTES: |

A B C D E F **G** H I J K L M N O P Q R S T U V W X Y Z

A B C D E F G **H** I J K L M N O P Q R S T U V W X Y Z

WEBSITE:

USERNAME:

PASSWORD:

PASSWORD:

EMAIL:

NOTES:

WEBSITE:

USERNAME:

PASSWORD:

PASSWORD:

EMAIL:

NOTES:

WEBSITE:

USERNAME:

PASSWORD:

PASSWORD:

EMAIL:

NOTES:

WEBSITE:	A
USERNAME:	B
PASSWORD:	C
PASSWORD:	D
EMAIL:	E
NOTES:	F

WEBSITE:

USERNAME:

PASSWORD:

PASSWORD:

EMAIL:

NOTES:

WEBSITE:

USERNAME:

PASSWORD:

PASSWORD:

EMAIL:

NOTES:

A B C D E F G H I J K L M N O P Q R S T U V W X Y Z

WEBSITE:

USERNAME:

PASSWORD:

PASSWORD:

EMAIL:

NOTES:

WEBSITE:

USERNAME:

PASSWORD:

PASSWORD:

EMAIL:

NOTES:

WEBSITE:

USERNAME:

PASSWORD:

PASSWORD:

EMAIL:

NOTES:

WEBSITE:

USERNAME:

PASSWORD:

PASSWORD:

EMAIL:

NOTES:

WEBSITE:

USERNAME:

PASSWORD:

PASSWORD:

EMAIL:

NOTES:

WEBSITE:

USERNAME:

PASSWORD:

PASSWORD:

EMAIL:

NOTES:

A
B
C
D
E
F
G
H
I
J
K
L
M
N
O
P
Q
R
S
T
U
V
W
X
Y
Z

A
B
C
D
E
F
G
H
I
J
K
L
M
N
O
P
Q
R
S
T
U
V
W
X
Y
Z

WEBSITE:

USERNAME:

PASSWORD:

PASSWORD:

EMAIL:

NOTES:

WEBSITE:

USERNAME:

PASSWORD:

PASSWORD:

EMAIL:

NOTES:

WEBSITE:

USERNAME:

PASSWORD:

PASSWORD:

EMAIL:

NOTES:

WEBSITE:

USERNAME:

PASSWORD:

PASSWORD:

EMAIL:

NOTES:

WEBSITE:

USERNAME:

PASSWORD:

PASSWORD:

EMAIL:

NOTES:

WEBSITE:

USERNAME:

PASSWORD:

PASSWORD:

EMAIL:

NOTES:

A B C D E F G H **I** J K L M N O P Q R S T U V W X Y Z

A B C D E F G H **I** J K L M N O P Q R S T U V W X Y Z

WEBSITE:

USERNAME:

PASSWORD:

PASSWORD:

EMAIL:

NOTES:

WEBSITE:

USERNAME:

PASSWORD:

PASSWORD:

EMAIL:

NOTES:

WEBSITE:

USERNAME:

PASSWORD:

PASSWORD:

EMAIL:

NOTES:

| WEBSITE: |
| USERNAME: |
| PASSWORD: |
| PASSWORD: |
| EMAIL: |
| NOTES: |

| WEBSITE: |
| USERNAME: |
| PASSWORD: |
| PASSWORD: |
| EMAIL: |
| NOTES: |

| WEBSITE: |
| USERNAME: |
| PASSWORD: |
| PASSWORD: |
| EMAIL: |
| NOTES: |

A B C D E F G H **I** J K L M N O P Q R S T U V W X Y Z

<table>
<tr><td rowspan="2">A
B
C
D
E
F
G
H
I
J
K
L
M
N
O
P
Q
R
S
T
U
V
W
X
Y
Z</td><td>WEBSITE:</td></tr>
</table>

WEBSITE:

USERNAME:

PASSWORD:

PASSWORD:

EMAIL:

NOTES:

WEBSITE:

USERNAME:

PASSWORD:

PASSWORD:

EMAIL:

NOTES:

WEBSITE:

USERNAME:

PASSWORD:

PASSWORD:

EMAIL:

NOTES:

WEBSITE:	
USERNAME:	
PASSWORD:	
PASSWORD:	
EMAIL:	
NOTES:	

WEBSITE:	
USERNAME:	
PASSWORD:	
PASSWORD:	
EMAIL:	
NOTES:	

WEBSITE:	
USERNAME:	
PASSWORD:	
PASSWORD:	
EMAIL:	
NOTES:	

A B C D E F G H I **J** K L M N O P Q R S T U V W X Y Z

A
B
C
D
E
F
G
H
I
J
K
L
M
N
O
P
Q
R
S
T
U
V
W
X
Y
Z

WEBSITE:

USERNAME:

PASSWORD:

PASSWORD:

EMAIL:

NOTES:

WEBSITE:

USERNAME:

PASSWORD:

PASSWORD:

EMAIL:

NOTES:

WEBSITE:

USERNAME:

PASSWORD:

PASSWORD:

EMAIL:

NOTES:

WEBSITE:

USERNAME:

PASSWORD:

PASSWORD:

EMAIL:

NOTES:

WEBSITE:

USERNAME:

PASSWORD:

PASSWORD:

EMAIL:

NOTES:

WEBSITE:

USERNAME:

PASSWORD:

PASSWORD:

EMAIL:

NOTES:

A B C D E F G H I J K L M N O P Q R S T U V W X Y Z

A
B
C
D
E
F
G
H
I
J
K
L
M
N
O
P
Q
R
S
T
U
V
W
X
Y
Z

WEBSITE:

USERNAME:

PASSWORD:

PASSWORD:

EMAIL:

NOTES:

WEBSITE:

USERNAME:

PASSWORD:

PASSWORD:

EMAIL:

NOTES:

WEBSITE:

USERNAME:

PASSWORD:

PASSWORD:

EMAIL:

NOTES:

WEBSITE:

USERNAME:

PASSWORD:

PASSWORD:

EMAIL:

NOTES:

WEBSITE:

USERNAME:

PASSWORD:

PASSWORD:

EMAIL:

NOTES:

WEBSITE:

USERNAME:

PASSWORD:

PASSWORD:

EMAIL:

NOTES:

A B C D E F G H I J **K** L M N O P Q R S T U V W X Y Z

A B C D E F G H I J **K** L M N O P Q R S T U V W X Y Z

WEBSITE:

USERNAME:

PASSWORD:

PASSWORD:

EMAIL:

NOTES:

WEBSITE:

USERNAME:

PASSWORD:

PASSWORD:

EMAIL:

NOTES:

WEBSITE:

USERNAME:

PASSWORD:

PASSWORD:

EMAIL:

NOTES:

WEBSITE:

USERNAME:

PASSWORD:

PASSWORD:

EMAIL:

NOTES:

WEBSITE:

USERNAME:

PASSWORD:

PASSWORD:

EMAIL:

NOTES:

WEBSITE:

USERNAME:

PASSWORD:

PASSWORD:

EMAIL:

NOTES:

A
B
C
D
E
F
G
H
I
J
K
L
M
N
O
P
Q
R
S
T
U
V
W
X
Y
Z

WEBSITE:

USERNAME:

PASSWORD:

PASSWORD:

EMAIL:

NOTES:

WEBSITE:

USERNAME:

PASSWORD:

PASSWORD:

EMAIL:

NOTES:

WEBSITE:

USERNAME:

PASSWORD:

PASSWORD:

EMAIL:

NOTES:

| WEBSITE: |
| USERNAME: |
| PASSWORD: |
| PASSWORD: |
| EMAIL: |
| NOTES: |

| WEBSITE: |
| USERNAME: |
| PASSWORD: |
| PASSWORD: |
| EMAIL: |
| NOTES: |

| WEBSITE: |
| USERNAME: |
| PASSWORD: |
| PASSWORD: |
| EMAIL: |
| NOTES: |

A B C D E F G H I J K **L** M N O P Q R S T U V W X Y Z

A
B
C
D
E
F
G
H
I
J
K
L
M
N
O
P
Q
R
S
T
U
V
W
X
Y
Z

WEBSITE:

USERNAME:

PASSWORD:

PASSWORD:

EMAIL:

NOTES:

WEBSITE:

USERNAME:

PASSWORD:

PASSWORD:

EMAIL:

NOTES:

WEBSITE:

USERNAME:

PASSWORD:

PASSWORD:

EMAIL:

NOTES:

WEBSITE:

USERNAME:

PASSWORD:

PASSWORD:

EMAIL:

NOTES:

WEBSITE:

USERNAME:

PASSWORD:

PASSWORD:

EMAIL:

NOTES:

WEBSITE:

USERNAME:

PASSWORD:

PASSWORD:

EMAIL:

NOTES:

A B C D E F G H I J K **L** M N O P Q R S T U V W X Y Z

A
B
C
D
E
F
G
H
I
J
K
L
M
N
O
P
Q
R
S
T
U
V
W
X
Y
Z

WEBSITE:

USERNAME:

PASSWORD:

PASSWORD:

EMAIL:

NOTES:

WEBSITE:

USERNAME:

PASSWORD:

PASSWORD:

EMAIL:

NOTES:

WEBSITE:

USERNAME:

PASSWORD:

PASSWORD:

EMAIL:

NOTES:

WEBSITE:		A
USERNAME:		B
PASSWORD:		C
PASSWORD:		D
EMAIL:		E
NOTES:		F

WEBSITE:		G
USERNAME:		H
PASSWORD:		I
PASSWORD:		J
EMAIL:		K
NOTES:		L

M

WEBSITE:		N
USERNAME:		O
PASSWORD:		P
PASSWORD:		Q
EMAIL:		R
NOTES:		S

T
U
V
W
X
Y
Z

A
B
C
D
E
F
G
H
I
J
K
L
M
N
O
P
Q
R
S
T
U
V
W
X
Y
Z

WEBSITE:

USERNAME:

PASSWORD:

PASSWORD:

EMAIL:

NOTES:

WEBSITE:

USERNAME:

PASSWORD:

PASSWORD:

EMAIL:

NOTES:

WEBSITE:

USERNAME:

PASSWORD:

PASSWORD:

EMAIL:

NOTES:

WEBSITE:

USERNAME:

PASSWORD:

PASSWORD:

EMAIL:

NOTES:

WEBSITE:

USERNAME:

PASSWORD:

PASSWORD:

EMAIL:

NOTES:

WEBSITE:

USERNAME:

PASSWORD:

PASSWORD:

EMAIL:

NOTES:

A
B
C
D
E
F
G
H
I
J
K
L
M
N
O
P
Q
R
S
T
U
V
W
X
Y
Z

WEBSITE:

USERNAME:

PASSWORD:

PASSWORD:

EMAIL:

NOTES:

WEBSITE:

USERNAME:

PASSWORD:

PASSWORD:

EMAIL:

NOTES:

WEBSITE:

USERNAME:

PASSWORD:

PASSWORD:

EMAIL:

NOTES:

| WEBSITE: |
| USERNAME: |
| PASSWORD: |
| PASSWORD: |
| EMAIL: |
| NOTES: |

| WEBSITE: |
| USERNAME: |
| PASSWORD: |
| PASSWORD: |
| EMAIL: |
| NOTES: |

| WEBSITE: |
| USERNAME: |
| PASSWORD: |
| PASSWORD: |
| EMAIL: |
| NOTES: |

A B C D E F G H I J K L M **N** O P Q R S T U V W X Y Z

WEBSITE:

USERNAME:

PASSWORD:

PASSWORD:

EMAIL:

NOTES:

WEBSITE:

USERNAME:

PASSWORD:

PASSWORD:

EMAIL:

NOTES:

WEBSITE:

USERNAME:

PASSWORD:

PASSWORD:

EMAIL:

NOTES:

WEBSITE:

USERNAME:

PASSWORD:

PASSWORD:

EMAIL:

NOTES:

WEBSITE:

USERNAME:

PASSWORD:

PASSWORD:

EMAIL:

NOTES:

WEBSITE:

USERNAME:

PASSWORD:

PASSWORD:

EMAIL:

NOTES:

A B C D E F G H I J K L M **N** O P Q R S T U V W X Y Z

A
B
C
D
E
F
G
H
I
J
K
L
M
N
O
P
Q
R
S
T
U
V
W
X
Y
Z

WEBSITE:

USERNAME:

PASSWORD:

PASSWORD:

EMAIL:

NOTES:

WEBSITE:

USERNAME:

PASSWORD:

PASSWORD:

EMAIL:

NOTES:

WEBSITE:

USERNAME:

PASSWORD:

PASSWORD:

EMAIL:

NOTES:

WEBSITE:

USERNAME:

PASSWORD:

PASSWORD:

EMAIL:

NOTES:

WEBSITE:

USERNAME:

PASSWORD:

PASSWORD:

EMAIL:

NOTES:

WEBSITE:

USERNAME:

PASSWORD:

PASSWORD:

EMAIL:

NOTES:

A B C D E F G H I J K L M N O P Q R S T U V W X Y Z

A
B
C
D
E
F
G
H
I
J
K
L
M
N
O
P
Q
R
S
T
U
V
W
X
Y
Z

WEBSITE:

USERNAME:

PASSWORD:

PASSWORD:

EMAIL:

NOTES:

WEBSITE:

USERNAME:

PASSWORD:

PASSWORD:

EMAIL:

NOTES:

WEBSITE:

USERNAME:

PASSWORD:

PASSWORD:

EMAIL:

NOTES:

WEBSITE:	
USERNAME:	
PASSWORD:	
PASSWORD:	
EMAIL:	
NOTES:	

WEBSITE:	
USERNAME:	
PASSWORD:	
PASSWORD:	
EMAIL:	
NOTES:	

WEBSITE:	
USERNAME:	
PASSWORD:	
PASSWORD:	
EMAIL:	
NOTES:	

A B C D E F G H I J K L M N **O** P Q R S T U V W X Y Z

WEBSITE:

USERNAME:

PASSWORD:

PASSWORD:

EMAIL:

NOTES:

WEBSITE:

USERNAME:

PASSWORD:

PASSWORD:

EMAIL:

NOTES:

WEBSITE:

USERNAME:

PASSWORD:

PASSWORD:

EMAIL:

NOTES:

| WEBSITE: |
| USERNAME: |
| PASSWORD: |
| PASSWORD: |
| EMAIL: |
| NOTES: |

| WEBSITE: |
| USERNAME: |
| PASSWORD: |
| PASSWORD: |
| EMAIL: |
| NOTES: |

| WEBSITE: |
| USERNAME: |
| PASSWORD: |
| PASSWORD: |
| EMAIL: |
| NOTES: |

A B C D E F G H I J K L M N O **P** Q R S T U V W X Y Z

A
B
C
D
E
F
G
H
I
J
K
L
M
N
O
P
Q
R
S
T
U
V
W
X
Y
Z

WEBSITE:

USERNAME:

PASSWORD:

PASSWORD:

EMAIL:

NOTES:

WEBSITE:

USERNAME:

PASSWORD:

PASSWORD:

EMAIL:

NOTES:

WEBSITE:

USERNAME:

PASSWORD:

PASSWORD:

EMAIL:

NOTES:

WEBSITE:

USERNAME:

PASSWORD:

PASSWORD:

EMAIL:

NOTES:

WEBSITE:

USERNAME:

PASSWORD:

PASSWORD:

EMAIL:

NOTES:

WEBSITE:

USERNAME:

PASSWORD:

PASSWORD:

EMAIL:

NOTES:

A B C D E F G H I J K L M N O **P** Q R S T U V W X Y Z

A
B
C
D
E
F
G
H
I
J
K
L
M
N
O
P
Q
R
S
T
U
V
W
X
Y
Z

WEBSITE:

USERNAME:

PASSWORD:

PASSWORD:

EMAIL:

NOTES:

WEBSITE:

USERNAME:

PASSWORD:

PASSWORD:

EMAIL:

NOTES:

WEBSITE:

USERNAME:

PASSWORD:

PASSWORD:

EMAIL:

NOTES:

WEBSITE:

USERNAME:

PASSWORD:

PASSWORD:

EMAIL:

NOTES:

WEBSITE:

USERNAME:

PASSWORD:

PASSWORD:

EMAIL:

NOTES:

WEBSITE:

USERNAME:

PASSWORD:

PASSWORD:

EMAIL:

NOTES:

A
B
C
D
E
F
G
H
I
J
K
L
M
N
O
P
Q
R
S
T
U
V
W
X
Y
Z

A
B
C
D
E
F
G
H
I
J
K
L
M
N
O
P
Q
R
S
T
U
V
W
X
Y
Z

WEBSITE:

USERNAME:

PASSWORD:

PASSWORD:

EMAIL:

NOTES:

WEBSITE:

USERNAME:

PASSWORD:

PASSWORD:

EMAIL:

NOTES:

WEBSITE:

USERNAME:

PASSWORD:

PASSWORD:

EMAIL:

NOTES:

WEBSITE:

USERNAME:

PASSWORD:

PASSWORD:

EMAIL:

NOTES:

WEBSITE:

USERNAME:

PASSWORD:

PASSWORD:

EMAIL:

NOTES:

WEBSITE:

USERNAME:

PASSWORD:

PASSWORD:

EMAIL:

NOTES:

A B C D E F G H I J K L M N O P Q R S T U V W X Y Z

A
B
C
D
E
F
G
H
I
J
K
L
M
N
O
P
Q
R
S
T
U
V
W
X
Y
Z

WEBSITE:

USERNAME:

PASSWORD:

PASSWORD:

EMAIL:

NOTES:

WEBSITE:

USERNAME:

PASSWORD:

PASSWORD:

EMAIL:

NOTES:

WEBSITE:

USERNAME:

PASSWORD:

PASSWORD:

EMAIL:

NOTES:

WEBSITE:

USERNAME:

PASSWORD:

PASSWORD:

EMAIL:

NOTES:

WEBSITE:

USERNAME:

PASSWORD:

PASSWORD:

EMAIL:

NOTES:

WEBSITE:

USERNAME:

PASSWORD:

PASSWORD:

EMAIL:

NOTES:

A
B
C
D
E
F
G
H
I
J
K
L
M
N
O
P
Q
R
S
T
U
V
W
X
Y
Z

WEBSITE:

USERNAME:

PASSWORD:

PASSWORD:

EMAIL:

NOTES:

WEBSITE:

USERNAME:

PASSWORD:

PASSWORD:

EMAIL:

NOTES:

WEBSITE:

USERNAME:

PASSWORD:

PASSWORD:

EMAIL:

NOTES:

WEBSITE:	
USERNAME:	
PASSWORD:	
PASSWORD:	
EMAIL:	
NOTES:	

WEBSITE:	
USERNAME:	
PASSWORD:	
PASSWORD:	
EMAIL:	
NOTES:	

WEBSITE:	
USERNAME:	
PASSWORD:	
PASSWORD:	
EMAIL:	
NOTES:	

A B C D E F G H I J K L M N O P Q **R** S T U V W X Y Z

<table>
<tr><td rowspan="26">A
B
C
D
E
F
G
H
I
J
K
L
M
N
O
P
Q
R
S
T
U
V
W
X
Y
Z</td></tr>
</table>

WEBSITE:

USERNAME:

PASSWORD:

PASSWORD:

EMAIL:

NOTES:

WEBSITE:

USERNAME:

PASSWORD:

PASSWORD:

EMAIL:

NOTES:

WEBSITE:

USERNAME:

PASSWORD:

PASSWORD:

EMAIL:

NOTES:

WEBSITE:

USERNAME:

PASSWORD:

PASSWORD:

EMAIL:

NOTES:

WEBSITE:

USERNAME:

PASSWORD:

PASSWORD:

EMAIL:

NOTES:

WEBSITE:

USERNAME:

PASSWORD:

PASSWORD:

EMAIL:

NOTES:

A B C D E F G H I J K L M N O P Q R **S** T U V W X Y Z

A
B
C
D
E
F
G
H
I
J
K
L
M
N
O
P
Q
R
S
T
U
V
W
X
Y
Z

WEBSITE:

USERNAME:

PASSWORD:

PASSWORD:

EMAIL:

NOTES:

WEBSITE:

USERNAME:

PASSWORD:

PASSWORD:

EMAIL:

NOTES:

WEBSITE:

USERNAME:

PASSWORD:

PASSWORD:

EMAIL:

NOTES:

WEBSITE:

USERNAME:

PASSWORD:

PASSWORD:

EMAIL:

NOTES:

WEBSITE:

USERNAME:

PASSWORD:

PASSWORD:

EMAIL:

NOTES:

WEBSITE:

USERNAME:

PASSWORD:

PASSWORD:

EMAIL:

NOTES:

A B C D E F G H I J K L M N O P Q R S T U V W X Y Z

A
B
C
D
E
F
G
H
I
J
K
L
M
N
O
P
Q
R
S
T
U
V
W
X
Y
Z

WEBSITE:

USERNAME:

PASSWORD:

PASSWORD:

EMAIL:

NOTES:

WEBSITE:

USERNAME:

PASSWORD:

PASSWORD:

EMAIL:

NOTES:

WEBSITE:

USERNAME:

PASSWORD:

PASSWORD:

EMAIL:

NOTES:

WEBSITE:

USERNAME:

PASSWORD:

PASSWORD:

EMAIL:

NOTES:

WEBSITE:

USERNAME:

PASSWORD:

PASSWORD:

EMAIL:

NOTES:

WEBSITE:

USERNAME:

PASSWORD:

PASSWORD:

EMAIL:

NOTES:

A B C D E F G H I J K L M N O P Q R S **T** U V W X Y Z

WEBSITE:

USERNAME:

PASSWORD:

PASSWORD:

EMAIL:

NOTES:

WEBSITE:

USERNAME:

PASSWORD:

PASSWORD:

EMAIL:

NOTES:

WEBSITE:

USERNAME:

PASSWORD:

PASSWORD:

EMAIL:

NOTES:

WEBSITE:

USERNAME:

PASSWORD:

PASSWORD:

EMAIL:

NOTES:

WEBSITE:

USERNAME:

PASSWORD:

PASSWORD:

EMAIL:

NOTES:

WEBSITE:

USERNAME:

PASSWORD:

PASSWORD:

EMAIL:

NOTES:

A B C D E F G H I J K L M N O P Q R S T U V W X Y Z

A
B
C
D
E
F
G
H
I
J
K
L
M
N
O
P
Q
R
S
T
U
V
W
X
Y
Z

WEBSITE:

USERNAME:

PASSWORD:

PASSWORD:

EMAIL:

NOTES:

WEBSITE:

USERNAME:

PASSWORD:

PASSWORD:

EMAIL:

NOTES:

WEBSITE:

USERNAME:

PASSWORD:

PASSWORD:

EMAIL:

NOTES:

WEBSITE:

USERNAME:

PASSWORD:

PASSWORD:

EMAIL:

NOTES:

WEBSITE:

USERNAME:

PASSWORD:

PASSWORD:

EMAIL:

NOTES:

WEBSITE:

USERNAME:

PASSWORD:

PASSWORD:

EMAIL:

NOTES:

A B C D E F G H I J K L M N O P Q R S T U V W X Y Z

A
B
C
D
E
F
G
H
I
J
K
L
M
N
O
P
Q
R
S
T
U
V
W
X
Y
Z

WEBSITE:

USERNAME:

PASSWORD:

PASSWORD:

EMAIL:

NOTES:

WEBSITE:

USERNAME:

PASSWORD:

PASSWORD:

EMAIL:

NOTES:

WEBSITE:

USERNAME:

PASSWORD:

PASSWORD:

EMAIL:

NOTES:

WEBSITE:

USERNAME:

PASSWORD:

PASSWORD:

EMAIL:

NOTES:

WEBSITE:

USERNAME:

PASSWORD:

PASSWORD:

EMAIL:

NOTES:

WEBSITE:

USERNAME:

PASSWORD:

PASSWORD:

EMAIL:

NOTES:

A B C D E F G H I J K L M N O P Q R S T U V W X Y Z

A
B
C
D
E
F
G
H
I
J
K
L
M
N
O
P
Q
R
S
T
U
V
W
X
Y
Z

WEBSITE:

USERNAME:

PASSWORD:

PASSWORD:

EMAIL:

NOTES:

WEBSITE:

USERNAME:

PASSWORD:

PASSWORD:

EMAIL:

NOTES:

WEBSITE:

USERNAME:

PASSWORD:

PASSWORD:

EMAIL:

NOTES:

| WEBSITE: |
| USERNAME: |
| PASSWORD: |
| PASSWORD: |
| EMAIL: |
| NOTES: |

| WEBSITE: |
| USERNAME: |
| PASSWORD: |
| PASSWORD: |
| EMAIL: |
| NOTES: |

| WEBSITE: |
| USERNAME: |
| PASSWORD: |
| PASSWORD: |
| EMAIL: |
| NOTES: |

A B C D E F G H I J K L M N O P Q R S T **U V** W X Y Z

A
B
C
D
E
F
G
H
I
J
K
L
M
N
O
P
Q
R
S
T
U
V
W
X
Y
Z

WEBSITE:

USERNAME:

PASSWORD:

PASSWORD:

EMAIL:

NOTES:

WEBSITE:

USERNAME:

PASSWORD:

PASSWORD:

EMAIL:

NOTES:

WEBSITE:

USERNAME:

PASSWORD:

PASSWORD:

EMAIL:

NOTES:

WEBSITE:

USERNAME:

PASSWORD:

PASSWORD:

EMAIL:

NOTES:

WEBSITE:

USERNAME:

PASSWORD:

PASSWORD:

EMAIL:

NOTES:

WEBSITE:

USERNAME:

PASSWORD:

PASSWORD:

EMAIL:

NOTES:

A B C D E F G H I J K L M N O P Q R S T U **V** W X Y Z

A
B
C
D
E
F
G
H
I
J
K
L
M
N
O
P
Q
R
S
T
U
V
W
X
Y
Z

WEBSITE:

USERNAME:

PASSWORD:

PASSWORD:

EMAIL:

NOTES:

WEBSITE:

USERNAME:

PASSWORD:

PASSWORD:

EMAIL:

NOTES:

WEBSITE:

USERNAME:

PASSWORD:

PASSWORD:

EMAIL:

NOTES:

WEBSITE:

USERNAME:

PASSWORD:

PASSWORD:

EMAIL:

NOTES:

WEBSITE:

USERNAME:

PASSWORD:

PASSWORD:

EMAIL:

NOTES:

WEBSITE:

USERNAME:

PASSWORD:

PASSWORD:

EMAIL:

NOTES:

A B C D E F G H I J K L M N O P Q R S T U V **W** X Y Z

WEBSITE:
USERNAME:
PASSWORD:
PASSWORD:
EMAIL:
NOTES:

WEBSITE:
USERNAME:
PASSWORD:
PASSWORD:
EMAIL:
NOTES:

WEBSITE:
USERNAME:
PASSWORD:
PASSWORD:
EMAIL:
NOTES:

WEBSITE:

USERNAME:

PASSWORD:

PASSWORD:

EMAIL:

NOTES:

WEBSITE:

USERNAME:

PASSWORD:

PASSWORD:

EMAIL:

NOTES:

WEBSITE:

USERNAME:

PASSWORD:

PASSWORD:

EMAIL:

NOTES:

A
B
C
D
E
F
G
H
I
J
K
L
M
N
O
P
Q
R
S
T
U
V
W
X
Y
Z

A
B
C
D
E
F
G
H
I
J
K
L
M
N
O
P
Q
R
S
T
U
V
W
X
Y
Z

WEBSITE:

USERNAME:

PASSWORD:

PASSWORD:

EMAIL:

NOTES:

WEBSITE:

USERNAME:

PASSWORD:

PASSWORD:

EMAIL:

NOTES:

WEBSITE:

USERNAME:

PASSWORD:

PASSWORD:

EMAIL:

NOTES:

	A
WEBSITE:	B
	C
USERNAME:	D
	E
PASSWORD:	F
	G
PASSWORD:	H
	I
EMAIL:	J
	K
NOTES:	L
	M
WEBSITE:	N
	O
USERNAME:	P
	Q
PASSWORD:	R
	S
PASSWORD:	T
	U
EMAIL:	V
	W
NOTES:	X
	Y
WEBSITE:	Z

WEBSITE:

USERNAME:

PASSWORD:

PASSWORD:

EMAIL:

NOTES:

WEBSITE:

USERNAME:

PASSWORD:

PASSWORD:

EMAIL:

NOTES:

WEBSITE:

USERNAME:

PASSWORD:

PASSWORD:

EMAIL:

NOTES:

A
B
C
D
E
F
G
H
I
J
K
L
M
N
O
P
Q
R
S
T
U
V
W
X
Y
Z

WEBSITE:

USERNAME:

PASSWORD:

PASSWORD:

EMAIL:

NOTES:

WEBSITE:

USERNAME:

PASSWORD:

PASSWORD:

EMAIL:

NOTES:

WEBSITE:

USERNAME:

PASSWORD:

PASSWORD:

EMAIL:

NOTES:

WEBSITE:

USERNAME:

PASSWORD:

PASSWORD:

EMAIL:

NOTES:

WEBSITE:

USERNAME:

PASSWORD:

PASSWORD:

EMAIL:

NOTES:

WEBSITE:

USERNAME:

PASSWORD:

PASSWORD:

EMAIL:

NOTES:

A B C D E F G H I J K L M N O P Q R S T U V W X Y Z

A
B
C
D
E
F
G
H
I
J
K
L
M
N
O
P
Q
R
S
T
U
V
W
X
Y
Z

WEBSITE:

USERNAME:

PASSWORD:

PASSWORD:

EMAIL:

NOTES:

WEBSITE:

USERNAME:

PASSWORD:

PASSWORD:

EMAIL:

NOTES:

WEBSITE:

USERNAME:

PASSWORD:

PASSWORD:

EMAIL:

NOTES:

WEBSITE:

USERNAME:

PASSWORD:

PASSWORD:

EMAIL:

NOTES:

WEBSITE:

USERNAME:

PASSWORD:

PASSWORD:

EMAIL:

NOTES:

WEBSITE:

USERNAME:

PASSWORD:

PASSWORD:

EMAIL:

NOTES:

A
B
C
D
E
F
G
H
I
J
K
L
M
N
O
P
Q
R
S
T
U
V
W
X
Y
Z

A
B
C
D
E
F
G
H
I
J
K
L
M
N
O
P
Q
R
S
T
U
V
W
X
Y
Z

WEBSITE:

USERNAME:

PASSWORD:

PASSWORD:

EMAIL:

NOTES:

WEBSITE:

USERNAME:

PASSWORD:

PASSWORD:

EMAIL:

NOTES:

WEBSITE:

USERNAME:

PASSWORD:

PASSWORD:

EMAIL:

NOTES:

WEBSITE:	A
USERNAME:	B
PASSWORD:	C
PASSWORD:	D
EMAIL:	E
NOTES:	F

WEBSITE:	G
USERNAME:	H
PASSWORD:	I
PASSWORD:	J
EMAIL:	K
NOTES:	L

WEBSITE:	M
USERNAME:	N
PASSWORD:	O
PASSWORD:	P
EMAIL:	Q
NOTES:	R

A B C D E F G H I J K L M N O P Q R S T U V W X Y **Z**

WEBSITE:

USERNAME:

PASSWORD:

PASSWORD:

EMAIL:

NOTES:

WEBSITE:

USERNAME:

PASSWORD:

PASSWORD:

EMAIL:

NOTES:

WEBSITE:

USERNAME:

PASSWORD:

PASSWORD:

EMAIL:

NOTES:

WEBSITE:

USERNAME:

PASSWORD:

PASSWORD:

EMAIL:

NOTES:

WEBSITE:

USERNAME:

PASSWORD:

PASSWORD:

EMAIL:

NOTES:

WEBSITE:

USERNAME:

PASSWORD:

PASSWORD:

EMAIL:

NOTES:

A B C D E F G H I J K L M N O P Q R S T U V W X Y Z

A
B
C
D
E
F
G
H
I
J
K
L
M
N
O
P
Q
R
S
T
U
V
W
X
Y
Z

WEBSITE:

USERNAME:

PASSWORD:

PASSWORD:

EMAIL:

NOTES:

WEBSITE:

USERNAME:

PASSWORD:

PASSWORD:

EMAIL:

NOTES:

WEBSITE:

USERNAME:

PASSWORD:

PASSWORD:

EMAIL:

NOTES:

| WEBSITE: |
| USERNAME: |
| PASSWORD: |
| PASSWORD: |
| EMAIL: |
| NOTES: |

| WEBSITE: |
| USERNAME: |
| PASSWORD: |
| PASSWORD: |
| EMAIL: |
| NOTES: |

| WEBSITE: |
| USERNAME: |
| PASSWORD: |
| PASSWORD: |
| EMAIL: |
| NOTES: |

A B C D E F G H I J K L M N O P Q R S T U V W X Y Z

NOTES

NOTES

NOTES

NOTES

NOTES

NOTES

I want to thank You

for purchasing This Book.

I would be very grateful

for taking a moment

and leaving feedback.

It helps our small business

grow and reach more people.